Mater Anserina

Mater Anserina

Poems in Latin for Children
with audio CD

Milena Minkova and Terence Tunberg

ISBN 978-1-58510-193-1

Printed in Canada

10 9 8 7 6 5 4 3 2 1

Table of Contents

Preface

The age of the songs and rhymes that circulate today under the title 'Mother Goose' is not securely established. It is clear that a good many of them already existed in the eighteenth century, a period when several printed collections were published. In our volume, we offer Latin versions of some of the best known rhymes and songs of this genre, both British and American. We not only hope that the Latin texts will provide delight, especially for the many people deeply familiar with the English songs since childhood, but will also help students of Latin develop their sense of the accentuation of Latin words. Teachers should have a special interest in this second goal, since accentuation, though just a part of pronunciation, is an important part.

The meters employed by the masters of classical Latin poetry, such as Vergil, Horace, and Ovid, are based on the quantity of syllables, namely regular sequences of long and short syllables. However, another system of Latin versification, which was based on word accent rather than syllable quantity, developed during the Middle Ages – a method of versification that had its origins in the later Roman empire, especially in the works of Christian authors. Accentual verse, which was frequently combined with rhyme in the final syllables of verses and sometimes also at the *caesurae* within verse-lines, reached a very sophisticated level by the eleventh and twelfth centuries, and has justly been called one of the great creative achievements of medieval Latin literature. This accentual and rhyming medieval Latin poetry was used for themes ranging from the light-hearted and jocular to the sacred: famous examples of it include the collection known as the *Carmina Burana* and the hymn *Stabat Mater*. Useful information about accentual Latin versification may be found in these two works:

> Charles H. Beeson, *A Primer of Medieval Latin. An Anthology of Prose and Poetry* (Chicago, 1926; repr. Washington D. C., 1986), pp. 314-82.

> Dag L. Norberg, *An Introduction to the Study of Medieval Latin Versification*, edited with introduction by Jan Ziolkowski, translated by Grant C. Roti and Jacqueline De La Chapelle Skubly (Washington D. C., 2004).

The medieval Latin verse-techniques based on sequences of word-accents and rhyme seem to us to offer the medium most appropriate for a Latin version of the 'Mother Goose' nursery rhymes. In fact, we have designed the verses in our *Mater Anserina* so that the natural accent of the Latin words coincides with the traditional melodies of the well-known songs or, in some cases, with the familiar rhythm of those nursery rhymes which are usually chanted or recited rather than sung. In this way the traditional melodies or rhythms can become a way to reinforce a student's sense of the accent in Latin words.

The following points are also worth observing about our Latin accentual verses.

1.) We not only employ the internal rhythms already familiar to those who know the English songs, we also make extensive use of end-rhyme. In most, but not absolutely every case, the abstract end-rhyme scheme in our Latin verses follows an order similar to that of the English original.

2.) There is no elision or aphaeresis in our verse, because we have composed each line so that a word ending in a vowel or –*m* preceded by a vowel is never directly followed by another word beginning with a vowel or with an –*h*.

3.) In a word of more than three syllables, we often allow a secondary accent. This is always separated by one syllable from the primary accent. In the case of a paroxytone, the secondary accent precedes, for example:

súntque **còndiméntis** *fáctae*

In the case of a proparoxytone, the secondary accent follows, for example:

sémper éam **séquitùr**

4.) When a monosyllable is preceded or followed by a polysyllable, the monosyllable can have an accent, but only if separated from the nearest accented syllable by at least one unaccented syllable, for example:

et dúlcibus **súnt**

or

pánem míhi **dés**

5.) When pair of monosyllables occurs, only one may have a primary stress, and this is typically the first one, for example:

quíd sis *nóbis núntià*

Each poem is followed by a list of words that the reader may not remember immediately.

Milena Minkova composed poems 2, 3, 6, 9, 10, 12, 13, 14, 15, 16, 18, 23, and Terence Tunberg composed poems 1, 4, 5, 7, 8, 11, 17, 19, 20, 21, 22, 24, 25, 26, 27, 28. However, both authors have benefitted, throughout the composition of the book, from their continuous mutual advice and support.

M.M. and T.T.
2005

Mater Anserina

Hey, diddle, diddle

Hey, diddle, diddle,
the cat and the fiddle,
the cow jumped over the moon.
The little dog laughed
to see such sport,
and the dish ran away with the spoon.

Somnium fallit

Sómnium fállit,
en féles hic psállit!
Praetérvolat lúnam nunc bós!
Canícula rídet
haec cónspicáns.
Fúgit trúlla cum lánce nunc nós.

---

bōs, bovis, *m.f.* – *ox, cow*
canīcula, ae, *f.* – *little dog*
cōnspicor, ārī, cōnspicātus sum – *to get sight of*
ēn – *lo and behold!*
fallō, ere, fefellī, falsum – *to deceive*
fēles, fēlis, *f.* – *cat*
fugiō, ere, fūgī + *accusative* – *to run away from somebody*

hīc (*adv.*) – *here*
lānx, lāncis, *f.* – *dish*
praetervolō, āre, āvī, ātum – *to fly by or past*
psallō, ere – *to play upon a stringed instrument*
somnium, ī, *n.* – *dream*
trūlla, ae, *f.* – *small ladle, spoon*

Mary had a little lamb

Mary had a little lamb,
little lamb,
little lamb,
Mary had a little lamb,
its fleece was white as snow.
Everywhere that Mary went,
Mary went,
Mary went,
everywhere that Mary went,
the lamb was sure to go.

It followed her to school one day,
school one day,
school one day,
it followed her to school one day,
which was against the rules.
It made the children laugh and
    play,
laugh and play,
laugh and play,
it made the children laugh and play,
to see a lamb at school.

And so the teacher turned it out,
turned it out,
turned it out,
and so the teacher turned it out,
but it still lingered near.
And waited patiently about,
patiently,
patiently,
and waited patiently about,
till Mary did appear.

Why does the lamb love Mary so,
Mary so,
Mary so,
why does the lamb love Mary so?
The eager children cried.
Well, Mary loves the lamb, you
    know,
lamb, you know,
lamb, you know,
well, Mary loves the lamb, you
    know,
the teacher did reply.

Agnicellum habuit Maria

Àgnicéllus cándidùs,
cándidùs,
cándidùs,
àgnicéllus cándidùs
Maríae cómes ít.
Sémper éam séquitùr,
séquitùr,
séquitùr,
sémper éam séquitùr,
María quóvis ít.

Còmitátus sémel ád,
sémel ád,
sémel ád,
còmitátus sémel ád
magístram schólae, tám
dèlectávit párvulòs,
párvulòs,
párvulòs,
dèlectávit párvulòs,
ut laúdent béstiàm.

Íre iússus ágnulùs,
ágnulùs,
ágnulùs,
íre iússus ágnulùs
a schólae dóminà,
mánsit támen sédulò,
sédulò,
sédulò,
mànsitúrus sédulò
cum cára sócià.

Èxclamárunt púerì,
púerì,
púerì,
èxclamárunt púerì:
"Maríam díligìt!"
"Ét haec ámat ágnulùm,
ágnulùm,
ágnulùm,
ét haec ámat ágnulùm,"
magístra réttulìt.

---

agnicellus, ī, m. – lambkin
bestia, ae, f. – beast, animal
candidus, a, um – snow-white
cārus, a, um – dear
comes, comitis, m. – companion
comitor, ārī, comitātus sum – to
   accompany
dēlectō, āre, āvī, ātum – to delight
dīligo, ere, dīlēxī, dīlectum – to be fond of,
   to love
domina, ae, f. – mistress
exclāmārunt = exclāmāvērunt

iubeō, ēre, iussī, iussum – to order
mānsitūrus, a, um – intending to stay
parvulī, ōrum, m. pl. – children
quōvīs – to wherever
referō, referre, rettulī, relātum – to reply
schola, ae, f. – school
sēdulō (adv.) – diligently
semel (adv.) – once
sequor, sequī, secūtus sum – to follow
socia, ae, f. – comrade, companion
tam… ut… – so… that…

Twinkle, twinkle, little star

Twinkle, twinkle, little star,
how I wonder what you are.
Up above the world so high,
like a diamond in the sky.
Twinkle, twinkle, little star,
how I wonder what you are.

Splende, splende, stellula

Splénde, splénde stéllulà,
quíd sis nóbis núntià.
Fìrmaménti támquam gémma
pèrornábis dìadéma.
Splénde, splénde stéllulà,
quíd sis nóbis núntià.

---

diadēma, diadēmatis, *n. – tiara, diadem*
firmāmentum, ī, *n. – the vault of heaven*
gemma, ae, *f. – gem*
nūntiō, āre, āvī, ātum – *to announce*
perōrnō, āre, āvī, ātum – *to adorn greatly*

splendeō, ēre – *to shine*
stellula, ae, *f. – little star*
*Note that the final -a in all these verses is
    short, except in the word* nūntiā.

Little Miss Muffet

Little Miss Muffet
sat on a tuffet
eating her curds and whey.
Along came a spider,
who sat down beside her
and frightened Miss Muffet away.

De parvula Bella

Párvula Bélla
sédit in sélla
sérum vel lác nunc ést.
Aránea sédit
cum Bélla nec édit,
sed Bélla regréssa tunc ést.

---

arānea, ae, *f. – spider*
Bella, ae, *f. – a female name from:*
    bellus, a, um *– nice*
edō, ere, ēdī, ēsum *– to eat*
ēst (*contracted form of* edit) *- s/he eats (not*
    to be confused with est)

lac, lactis, *n. – milk*
parvulus, a, um *– very little*
regredior, regredī, regressus sum *– to*
    retreat
sella, ae, *f. – seat*
serum, ī, *n. – whey*

Here we go 'round the mulberry bush

Here we go 'round the mulberry
    bush,
the mulberry bush,
the mulberry bush,
here we go 'round the mulberry
    bush,
so early in the morning.

These are the chores we'll do this
    week,
do this week,
do this week,
these are the chores we'll do this
    week,
so early every morning.

This is the way we wash our clothes,
wash our clothes
wash our clothes,
this is the way we wash our clothes,
so early Monday morning.

This is the way we iron our clothes,
iron our clothes,
iron our clothes,
this is the way we iron our clothes,
so early Tuesday morning.

This is the way we scrub the floor,
scrub the floor,
scrub the floor,
this is the way we scrub the floor,
so early Wednesday morning.

This is the way we mend our
    clothes,
mend our clothes,
mend our clothes,
this is the way we mend our clothes,
so early Thursday morning.

This is the way we sweep the floor,
sweep the floor,
sweep the floor,
this is the way we sweep the floor,
so early Friday morning.

This is the way we bake our bread,
bake our bread,
bake our bread,
this is the way we bake our bread,
so early Saturday morning.

This is the way we get dressed up,
get dressed up,
get dressed up,
this is the way we get dressed up,
so early Sunday morning.

Circa morum illam

Frúticem círca cúrrimus iám,
cúrrimus iám,
cúrrimus iám,
ín quo sunt móra sápida iám,
sub ípsam lúcem prímam.

Múnera núnc hebdómadis súnt,
hebdómadis súnt,
hebdómadis súnt,
múnera núnc hebdómadis súnt,
tam máne quóque díe.

Síc sunt lavándae véstes híc,
véstes híc,
véstes híc,
síc sunt lavándae véstes híc,
tam máne Lúnae díe.

Férro preménda líntea súnt,
líntea súnt,
líntea súnt,
férro preménda líntea súnt,
tam máne Mártis díe.

Sólum purgándum nóbis est núnc,
nóbis est núnc,
nóbis est núnc,

sólum purgándum nóbis est núnc,
cum súrgit Máia nátus.

Síc vestiménta súimus núnc,
súimus núnc,
súimus núnc,
síc vestiménta súimus núnc,
tam máne Ióvis díe.

Síc paviménta vérrimus núnc,
vérrimus núnc,
vérrimus núnc,
síc paviménta vérrimus núnc,
cum máne Vénus súrgit.

Pánes coquéndi clíbano súnt,
clíbano súnt,
clíbano súnt,
pánes coquéndi clíbano súnt,
Satúrni díe máne.

Síc exornári décet iam nós,
décet iam nós,
décet iam nós,
síc exornári décet iam nós,
tam máne Sólis díe.

---

clībanus, ī, n. – *portable oven for bread*
coquō, ere, coxī, coctum – *to cook, to bake*
decet, ēre, decuit – *it is becoming, it is
    proper*
ferrum, ī, n. – *iron*
frutex, fruticis, m. – *bush*
hebdomas, hebdomadis, f. – *week*
Iovis diēs – *Thursday (the day of Jupiter)*
lavō, āre, lāvī, lōtum – *to wash*
linteum, ī, n. – *linen*
Lūnae diēs – *Monday (the day of the Moon)*
Māiā nātus – *the son of the nymph Maia,
    Mercury (diēs Mercuriī – Wednesday)*
māne (adv.) – *early in the morning*
Martis diēs – *Tuesday (the day of Mars)*
mōrum, ī, n. – *mulberry*
mōrus, ī, f. – *a mulberry tree or shrub*

mūnus, mūneris, n. – *duty, chore*
pānis, pānis, m. – *bread*
pavīmentum, ī, n. – *floor*
premō, ere, pressī, pressum – *to press*
pūrgō, āre, āvī, ātum – *to clean*
sapidus, a, um – *luscious, delicious*
Sāturnī diēs– *Saturday (the day of Saturn)*
Sōlis diēs – *Sunday (the day of the Sun)*
solum, ī, n. – *ground, floor*
suō, ere, suī, sūtum – *to sew*
surgō, ere, surrēxī, surrēctum – *to rise*
Venus, Veneris, f. – *Venus* (diēs Veneris
    – Friday)
verrō, ere, verrī, versum – *to sweep*
vestīmentum, ī, n. – *clothing*
vestis, vestis, f. – *garment*

13

Itsy bitsy spider

Itsy bitsy spider
climbed up the water spout,
down came the rain
and washed the spider out;
up came the sun
and dried up all the rain,
and the itsy bitsy spider
climbed up the spout again.

De parva aranea textrice

Écce téxtrix párva
subívit fístulàm.
Plúvia túnc
exégit párvulàm.
Látices sól
siccávit dúlcitèr.
Téxtrix rúrsus túbum síccum
subívit návitèr.

---

arānea, ae, *f.* – *spider*
dulciter (*adv.*) – *gently*
exigō, ere, exēgī, exāctum – *to drive out*
ecce – *lo and behold!*
fistula, ae, *f.* – *water-pipe*
latex, laticis, *m.* – *liquid, water*
nāviter (*adv.*) – *diligently*
parvulus, a, um – *rather small*
pluvia, ae, *f.* – *rain*

rūrsus (*adv.*) – *again*
siccō, āre, āvī, ātum – *to dry*
siccus, a, um – *dry*
sōl, sōlis, *m.* – *sun*
subeō, subīre, subīvī, subitum – *to go up to*
textrīx, textrīcis, *f.* – *weaver, (figuratively)
  spider*
tubus, ī, *m.* – *tube, pipe*

It's raining, it's pouring

It's raining, it's pouring,
the old man is snoring.
Bumped his head
and he went to bed
and he couldn't get up in the morning.
Rain, rain, go away;
come again another day;
little Johnny wants to play.

Non imber abivit

Non ímber abívit,
hic sénex dormívit.
Cápitè,
laésus cápitè
se leváre máne nequívit.
Nunc, nunc ábeàt,
ímber né revéniàt!
Lúsum púer éxeàt!

---

abeō, abīre, abīvī, abitum – *to go away*
caput, capitis, *n.* – *head*
dormiō, īre, īvī, ītum – *to sleep*
imber, imbris, *m.* – *rain*
laedō, ere, laesī, laesum – *to hurt*
levō, āre, āvī, ātum – *to lift up*

lūsum exīre – *to go out to play*
māne (*adv.*) – *in the morning*
nequeō, īre, nequīvī – *not to be able*
reveniō, īre, revēnī, reventum – *to come back*
senex, senis, *m.* – *old man*

Hot cross buns

Hot cross buns!
Hot cross buns!
Hot cross buns!
One a penny, two a penny,
Hot cross buns!
Hot cross buns!
Hot cross buns!
If you have no daughters,
give them to your sons!

Crustula decussata

Párvulà
crústulà,
dècussáta iám paráta.
Párvulà.

Crústulà
párvulà.
Párvo cónstant. Fóris próstant
crústulà.

Párvulà
crústulà.
Fìliábus sí tu cáres,
mèreántur líba máres.
Crústulà!

---

careō, ēre, caruī + *ablative – to lack
    something*
parvō cōnstāre – *to have a little cost*
crūstulum, ī, *n. – cookie, bun*
decussātus, a, um – *crossed, wearing a
    cross*
fīliābus = fīliīs (*feminine*)

forīs (*adv.*) – *outside*
lībum, ī, *n. – bun*
mās, maris, *m. – male*
mereō, ēre, meruī, meritum – *to deserve*
parvulus, a, um – *rather small*
prōstō, āre, prōstitī – *to be exposed for sale*

Jack and Jill

Jack and Jill
went up the hill
to fetch a pail of water.
Jack fell down
and broke his crown
and Jill came tumbling after.
Up Jack got
and home did trot
as fast as he could caper.
Went to bed
and plastered his head
with vinegar and brown paper.

De Iuliana et de Ioanne

Túmulùm
scandébant túm
Ioánnes, Iùliána.
Púer ít,
sed cécidìt.
Hi rédeùnt ad plána.

Púerùm
redúxit túm
puélla cómes sána.
Dátur núnc
quod fóvet húnc
acétum cúm membrána.

---

acētum, ī, *n.* – *vinegar*
comes, comitis, *m. f.* – *companion*
foveō, ēre, fōvī, fōtum – *to cherish, to foment*
membrāna, ae, *f.* – *parchment*
plānum, ī, *n.* – *level ground*

redūcō, ere, redūxī, reductum – *to lead back*
sānus, a, um – *in good health*
scandō, ere – *to climb*
tumulus, ī, *m.* – *hill*

Little Bo Peep

Little Bo Peep has lost her sheep
and can't tell where to find them.
Leave them alone, and they'll come home,
wagging their tails behind them.

De garrula parvula

Pécus amíssum gárrulà
puélla pèrquisívit.
Nóli dolére, párvulà;
títubans gréx redíbit.

āmittō, ere, āmīsī, āmissum – *to lose*
garrulus, a, um – *chattering*
grex, gregis, *m.* – *flock*
parvulus, a, um – *very small*

pecus, pecoris, *n.* – *cattle, sheep*
perquīrō, ere, perquīsīvī, perquīsītum – *to make a diligent search*
titubō, āre, āvī, ātum – *to stagger, to totter*

Little Boy Blue

Little Boy Blue, come blow your horn,
the sheep's in the meadow, the cow's in the corn.
Where is the boy who looks after the sheep?
He's under a haycock fast asleep.
Will you wake him? No, not I.
For if I do, he's sure to cry.

De puerulo coloris caerulei

Cáne nunc, púer, tíbiìs:
sunt óves et váccae nunc ágris in hís.
Púer qui séquitur pécudes hás,
deféssus petívit ténebràs.
Íbi díu iáceàt,
ne sómnum rúptum défleàt!

---

caeruleus, a, um – *blue*
canō, ere, cecinī, cantum – *to sing*
color, colōris, *m.* – *color*
dēfessus, a, um – *tired*
dēfleō, ēre, dēflēvī, dēflētum – *to weep over*
iaceō, ēre, iacuī – *to lie*
ovis, ovis, *f.* – *sheep*
pecus, pecudis, *f.* – *a head of cattle, one of a flock*

puerulus, ī, *m.* – *little boy*
rumpō, ere, rūpī, ruptum – *to break*
sequor, sequī, secūtus sum – *to follow*
somnus, ī, *m.* – *sleep*
tenebrae, ārum, *f.pl.* – *shade*
tībia, ae, *f.* (also *pl.*) – *pipe, flute*
vacca, ae, f. – *cow*

25

Georgie Porgie

Georgie Porgie, puddin' and pie,
kissed the girls and made them cry.
When the boys came out to play,
Georgie Porgie ran away.

De Georgio

Tót puéllis óscula dás,
quárum vídes lácrimàs.
Púeròs cur aúfugìs?
Ó Geórgi, métuìs!

---

aufugiō, ere, aufūgī – *to run away from*
metuō, ere, metuī – *to be afraid of*

ōsculum, ī, *n.* – *kiss*
tot (*adv.*) – *so many*

27

Humpty Dumpty

Humpty Dumpty sat on a wall,
Humpty Dumpty had a great fall.
All the king's horses, and all the king's men,
couldn't put Humpty together again.

De Humphrido Dumphrido

Múro laéte séderat híc.
Át nunc praéceps cécidit síc,
út nec minístri sint régii quí
Húmphridum iúvent nec équites hí.

---

at – *but*
eques, equitis, *m.* – *cavalryman*
hīc *(adv.)* – *here*
iuvō, āre, iūvī, iūtum – *to help*
laetē *(adv.)* – *joyfully*

minister, ministrī, *m.* – *attendant*
mūrus, ī, *m.* – *wall*
praeceps, praecipitis – *headlong*
rēgius, a, um – *royal*

Hickory, dickory, dock

Hickory, dickory, dock,
the mouse ran up the clock.
The clock struck one,
the mouse ran down!
Hickory, dickory, dock.

Vox horarum

Músculum cóncitat vóx
horárum; pétit móx
clepsýdram quaé
tinnívit túnc.
Músculus fúgitat núnc.

---

clepsydra, ae, *f. – clock (a water clock). This
Greek word is accented on the penult.*
concitō, āre, āvī, ātum – *to rouse*
fugito, āre, āvī – *to flee in haste*
hōra, ae, *f. – hour*

*Note the difference in vowel sound between
vōx and mox.*
mūsculus, ī, *m. – a little mouse*
petō, ere, petīvī, petītum – *to attempt to
go to*
tinniō, īre, īvī, ītum – *to make a sound*

Pat-a-cake, pat-a-cake

Pat-a-cake, pat-a-cake, baker's man,
bake me a cake as fast as you can.
Roll it, and prick it, and mark it with a "B"
and put it in the oven for Baby and me!

Massam depsas

Súbige mássam celérrimè!
Dépsito mássam, púer, pro mé.
Vólvito, fódito: torreátur sát.
In crústa nómen párvuli pósitum stát.

---

celerrimē (*adv.*) – *very fast*
crūsta, ae, *f.* – *crust*
depsitō – *future active imperative 2p. sg.*
depsō, ere, depsuī, depstum – *to knead*
fodiō, ere, fōdī, fossum – *to dig*
foditō – *future active imperative 2p. sg.*
massa, ae, *f.* – *dough*

parvulus, ī, *m.* – *a little boy*
sat (*adv.*) – *enough*
subigō, ere, subēgī, subāctum – *to
    dominate, to break up, to knead*
torreō, ēre, torruī, tostum – *to bake*
volvitō – *future active imperative 2p. sg.*
volvō, ere, volvī, volūtum – *to turn*

Ride a cock-horse

Ride a cock-horse to Banbury Cross,
to see a fine lady upon a white horse;
rings on her fingers and bells on her toes,
and she shall have music wherever she goes.

Equita Bannavenum

Sí Bannavénum vénies móx
harúndine véctus ut éques, haec vóx
é tintinnábulis íbit ad té.
Nam dómina nóbilis órnat his sé!

Bannāvēnum, ī, n. – *Banbury Cross*
domina, ae, *f.* – *lady*
eques, equitis, *m.* – *rider*
equitō, āre, āvī, ātum – *to ride*
harundō, harundinis, *f.* – *cock-horse*
nōbilis, nōbile – *noble*
ōrnō, āre, āvī, ātum – *to adorn*

tintinnabulum, ī, n. – *bell, ring*
ut – *as*
vehō, ere, vēxī, vectum – *to carry, to bear*;
    passive – *to ride*
Note the difference in vowel sound between
    mox *and* vōx.

She'll be coming round the mountain

She'll be coming round the mountain,
when she comes.
She'll be coming round the mountain,
when she comes.
She'll be coming round the mountain,
she'll be coming round the mountain,
she'll be coming round the mountain,
when she comes.

She'll be driving six white horses,
when she comes.
She'll be driving six white horses,
when she comes.
She'll be driving six white horses,
she'll be driving six white horses,
she'll be driving six white horses,
when she comes.

Oh, we'll all go out to greet her,
when she comes.
Oh, we'll all go out to greet her,
when she comes.
Oh, we'll all go out to greet her,
oh, we'll all go out to greet her,
oh, we'll all go out to greet her,
when she comes.

Circa montem ducetur

Círca móntem mox ducétur:
íbit húc.
Círca móntem mox ducétur:
íbit húc.
Círca móntem mox ducétur,
círca móntem mox ducétur,
círca móntem mox ducétur:
íbit húc.

Álbis équis sex vehétur:
íbit húc.
Álbis équis sex vehétur:
íbit húc.
Álbis équis sex vehétur,
álbis équis sex vehétur,
álbis équis sex vehétur:
íbit húc.

Túnc a nóbis salutétur:
íbit húc.
Túnc a nóbis salutétur:
íbit húc.
Túnc a nóbis salutétur,
túnc a nóbis salutétur,
túnc a nóbis salutétur:
íbit húc!

---

albus, a, um – *white*
equus, ī, *m.* – *horse*
hūc (*adv.*) – *to this place*

salūtō, āre, āvī, ātum – *to greet*
vehō, ere, vēxī, vectum – *to bear*; passive
– *to ride*

Ring a-round the roses

Ring a-round the roses,
a pocket full of posies.
A-tishoo! A-tishoo!
We all fall down.

Rosas circum ite

Mánibus coniúncti
nunc rósas círcum cúncti
cúrrite! Cúrrite!
Consístitè!

---

coniungō, ere, coniūnxī, coniūnctum – *to join*

cōnsistō, ere, cōnstitī – *to stand still*
cūnctus, a, um – *all together*

Doctor Foster

Doctor Foster went to Gloucester
in a shower of rain.
He stepped in a puddle
right up to his middle,
and never went there again.

De medico Festo

Féstum scímus ísse Séstum.
Féstus médicus ést.
Et ímbre conspérsus,
lumbístenus mérsus,
illúc non revérsus ést.

---

cōnspergō, ere, cōnspersī, cōnspersum – *to*
    sprinkle, to moisten
Festus, ī, *m. – a name of a man*
illūc (*adv.*) – *to that place*
imber, imbris, *m. – rain*
lumbus, ī, *m. – loin*

medicus, ī, *m. – doctor*
mergō, ere, mersī, mersum – *to dip, to sink*
revertor, revertī, reversus – *to return*
Sēstus, ī, *f. – a name of a town*
tenus + *ablative* (postposition) – *up to*

Star light, star bright

Star light, star bright,
first star I see tonight,
I wish I may, I wish I might,
have the wish I wish tonight.

Stellula princeps

Míca, míca,
Prínceps tu stéllulà!
Quod péto fác ut vídeàm:
Dónum dés ut hábeàm!

---

fac ut + *subjunctive… – see to it that…*
micō, āre – *to gleam*
prīnceps, prīncipis – *first*
stellula, ae, *f. – little star*

ut – *in order that*
*Note that the first line ends in a long -ā,
    and the second in a short -a.*

What are little boys made of? … What are little girls made of?

What are little boys made of?
Snips and snails,
and puppy dog's tails:
that's what little boys are made of!

What are little girls made of?
Sugar and spice,
and everything nice:
that's what little girls are made of!

Unde pueruli et puellulae facti?

Únde púeri fácti?
Frústis súnt,
et cóchleis súnt,
súntque cánum caúdis fácti!

Únde párvulae fáctae?
Sáccharo súnt,
et dúlcibus súnt,
súntque còndiméntis fáctae!

---

canis, canis, *m. – dog*
cauda, ae, *f. – tail*
cochlea, ae, *f. – snail*
condīmentum, ī, *n. – spice*
dulcia, ium, *n. pl. – sweet things, sweets*
frūstum, ī, *n. – piece*

parvula, ae, *f. – little girl*
puellula, ae, *f. – little girl*
puerulus, ī, *m. – little boy*
saccharum, ī, *n. – sugar*
unde *– from where?*

Simple Simon

Simple Simon met a pieman,
going to the fair.
Said Simple Simon to the pieman,
"Let me taste your ware."

Said the pieman unto Simon,
"Show me first your penny."
Said Simple Simon to the pieman,
"Indeed I have not any."

Simple Simon went a-fishing,
for to catch a whale;
but all the water he had got
was in his mother's pail.

Simple Simon went to look,
if plums grew on a thistle;
he pricked his fingers very much,
which made poor Simon whistle.

He went for water in a sieve,
but soon it all fell through;
and now poor Simple Simon
bids you all adieu.

De Sardo Bardo

Pístor Sárdum vídit Bárdum
vénditúrus rés.
Tunc aúdit Sárdum pístor
    Bárdum:
"Pánem míhi dés!"

Pístor Sárdo díxit Bárdo:
"Númmus détur míhi plénus."
Respónsum túnc est hóc a
    Bárdo:
"Quid dábo síc egénus?"

Sárdus Bárdus ít piscátum
cétum cúpièns.
Sed áqua dátur únde víx
quid súmat sítièns.

Sárdus Bárdus ít spectátum
num dúmus álat prúnum.
Sed únguem spína púnctum
tunc hábuìt non únum.

Petívit áquam críbro, séd
efflúxit áqua túnc.
Miséllus Sárdus Bárdus
'vále' dícit núnc!

---

alō, ere, aluī, altum/alitum – *to nourish*
bardus, a, um – *dull of apprehension*
cētus, ī, m. – *any large sea-animal, whale*
crībrum, ī, n. – *sieve*
dūmus, ī, m. – *thorn-bush*
effluō, ere, efflūxī – *to flow away*
egēnus, a, um – *poor*
īre piscātum – *to go fishing*
īre spectātum – *to go look carefully*
misellus, a, um – *wretched*
num – *if, whether*
nummus, ī, m. – *coin, payment*
pānis, pānis, m. – *bread*
piscor, ārī, piscātus sum – *to fish*
pīstor, pīstōris, m. – *baker*

plēnus, a, um – *full*
prūnum, ī, n. – *plum*
pungō, ere, pupugī, pūnctum – *to pierce*
Sardus, ī, m. – *a personal name; Sardus*
    means also an inhabitant of the
    island of Sardinia (in ancient times
    the Sardinians were known for their
    faithlessness)
sitiō, īre, īvī – *to be thirsty*
spectō, āre, āvī, ātum – *to look carefully*
spīna, ae, f. – *thorn*
unde – *from where*
unguis, unguis, m. – *nail*
vēndō, ere, vēndidī, vēnditum – *to sell*
vix (adv.) – *hardly*

Hush, little baby

Hush, little baby, don't say a word,
papa's gonna buy you a mockingbird.

If that mockingbird don't sing,
papa's gonna buy you a diamond ring.

If that diamond ring turns brass,
papa's gonna buy you a looking glass.

If that looking glass gets broke,
papa's gonna buy you a billy goat.

If that billy goat don't pull,
papa's gonna buy you a cart and bull.

If that cart and bull turn over,
papa's gonna buy you a dog named Rover.

And if that dog named Rover won't bark.
papa's gonna to buy you a horse and cart.

And if that horse and cart fall down,
you'll still be the sweetest little baby in town.

Tace infans!

Ínfans silébis; táceas iám:
páter ávem pórriget gárrulàm.

Ávis sí non gárrièt,
gémmam pró te páter invénièt.

Gémma túnc si fíet aés,
dábit vítrum quód tunc
    inspíciès.

Sí frangátur spéculùm,
cáprum páter áfferat
    párvulùm.

Huíc aráre nón est mós?
Cápri lóco póterit émi bós!

Cúrrus sí tunc dèstruétur,
cánis Árgus ílico tíbi détur.

Et Árgi sí non pérstrepet vóx,
équis bígae iúnctae dabúntur
    móx.

Et équum sí perdíderis,
tú dulcíssimùs tum
    permánserìs!

---

aes, aeris, *n.* – *bronze*
afferō, afferre, attulī, allātum – *to bring*
Argus, ī, *m.* – *name of a dog*
arō, āre, āvī, ātum – *to plough*
avis, avis, *f.* – *bird*
bīgae, ārum, *f.pl.* – *chariot*
bōs, bovis, *m. f.* – *ox*
canis, canis, *m.f.* – *dog*
caper, caprī, *m.* – *goat*
currus, ūs, *m.* – *chariot*
dēstruō, ere, destrūxī, dēstrūctum – *to tear down*
dulcissimus, a, um – *sweetest*
emō, ere, ēmī, ēmptum – *to buy*
equus, ī, *m.* – *horse*
frangō, ere, frēgī, frāctum – *to break*
garriō, īre, īvī, ītum – *to chatter*
garrulus, a, um – *chattering*
gemma, ae, *f.* – *gem, jewel*
īlicō (*adv.*) – *on the spot*

īnfāns, īnfantis, *m.f.* – *baby*
iungō, ere, iūnxī, iūnctum – *to yoke*
inspiciō, ere, inspexī, inspectum – *to look into*
locō + *genitive* – *in the place of*
mōs, mōris, *m.* – *custom*
parvulus, a, um – *little*
perdō, ere, perdidī, perditum – *to lose*
permaneō, ēre, permānsī – *to remain to the end*
perstrepō, ere, perstrepuī, perstrepitum – *to make much noise*
porrigō, ere, porrēxī, porrēctum – *to offer, to grant*
sileō, ēre, siluī – *to be silent*
speculum, ī, *n.* – *mirror*
taceō, ēre, tacuī, tacitum – *to be silent*
vitrum, ī, *n.* – *glass, mirror*
Note the difference in vowel sound between vōx *and* mox.

One, two, buckle my shoe

1,2
One, two buckle my shoe;
3,4
Three, four, knock at the door;
5,6
Five, six, pick up sticks;
7,8
Seven, eight, lay them straight;
9,10
Nine, ten, a good fat hen.

Semel, bis…

Sémel cómede mél.
Túndis óstium bís:
fác ter návitèr.
Quáter nunc lígna fér.
Caédes haec quínquiès.
Rádes haec séxiès.
Pónes haec séptiès.
Stérnes haec óctiès.
Nóvies púllos dés:
cóques hos déciès!

---

bis (*adv.*) – *twice*
caedō, ere, cecīdī, caesum – *to cut*
comedō, ere, comēdī, comēsum – *to eat*
coquō, ere, coxī, coctum – *to cook*
deciēs (*adv.*) – *ten times*
lignum, ī, *n.* – *wood*
mel, mellis, *n.* – *honey*
nāviter (*adv.*) – *diligently*
noviēs (*adv.*) – *nine times*
octiēs (*adv.*) – *eight times*
ostium, ī, *n.* – *door*

pullus, ī, *m.* – *chicken*
quater (*adv.*) – *four times*
quīnquiēs (*adv.*) – *five times*
rādō, ere, rāsī, rāsum – *to scrape*
semel (*adv.*) – *once*
septiēs (*adv.*) – *seven times*
sexiēs (*adv.*) – *six times*
sternō, ere, strāvī, strātum – *to spread*
ter (*adv.*) – *three times*
tundō, ere, tutudī, tūnsum/tūsum – *to strike*

Pussycat, pussycat

Pussycat, pussycat, where have you been?
"I've been to London to visit the queen."
Pussycat, pussycat, what did you there?
"I frightened a little mouse under her chair."

O, feles, feles

Úrbem cur víseris, féles, mi díc.
"Regínam vísi, quae vívit illíc."
Quíd apud éam pelléxit sic té?
"Mus érat íbi, qui tímuit mé!"

---

fēles, fēlis, *f.* – *cat*
illīc (*adv.*) – *there*
mī = mihi
mūs, mūris, *m.* – *mouse*
pelliciō, ere, pellexī, pellectum – *to attract*

regīna, ae, *f.* – *queen*
timeō, ēre, timuī – *to fear*
urbs, urbis, *f.* – *city; the city of London*
vīso, ere, vīsī, vīsum – *to visit*

A man in the wilderness

A man in the wilderness
asked this of me:
"How many strawberries
grow in the sea?"
I answered him
as I thought good:
"As many red herrings
as swim in the wood."

Aenigma

In sílvis vir rústicùs
ádiit mé:
"Mári quot frága súnt?
Rógito té."
Vérba tunc haéc
réttuli síc:
"Tot mári sunt frága
quot písces sunt híc."

---

adeō, adīre, adīvī, aditum – *to approach*
aenigma, aenigmatis, *n.* – *riddle*
frāgum, ī, *n.* – *strawberry*
hīc (*adv.*) – *here*
piscis, piscis, *m.* – *fish*
quot – *as many*
quot? – *how many?*

referō, referre, rettulī, relātum – *to reply*
rogitō, āre, āvī, ātum – *to ask with*
  eagerness
rūsticus, a, um – *belonging to the country,*
  rustic
silva, ae, *f.* – *forest*
tot – *so many*

Oh, the grand old Duke of York

Oh, the grand old Duke of York,
he had ten thousand men;
he marched them up to the top of the hill,
and he marched them down again.
And, when they were up they were up;
and when they were down they were down.
But when they were only halfway up,
they were neither up nor down.

De duce Eboracensi

Túnc Ebòracénsis dúx
ascéndit clívum húnc
cum décem mílitum mílibus quós
hinc deórsum dúxit túnc.
Venérunt tum cámpos in hós:
ivérunt tum clívum in húnc.
Cum médium lócum nácti súnt,
érant neútro lóco túnc!

---

ascendō, ere, ascendī, ascēnsum – *to climb*
campus, ī, *m.* – *field*
clīvus, ī, *m.* – *hill*
decem mīlia + *genitive* – *ten thousand*
deorsum (*adv.*) – *downward*
Eborācēnsis, Eborācēnse – *related to York*
   (Eborācum, ī, *n.*)

hinc (*adv.*) – *from here*
medius, a, um – *middle*
mīles, mīlitis, *m.* – *soldier*
nancīscor, nancīscī, nactus/nanctus sum
   – *to stumble on, to find*
neuter, neutra, neutrum – *neither of two*

Yankee Doodle

Yankee Doodle came to town,
a-riding on a pony;
he stuck a feather in his hat
and called it macaroni.

Yankee Doodle keep it up,
Yankee Doodle dandy;
mind the music and the steps
and with the girls be handy.

Father and I went down to camp,
along with Cap'n Goodwin:
the men and boys all stood around
as thick as hasty puddin'.

Yankee Doodle keep it up,
Yankee Doodle dandy;
mind the music and the steps
and with the girls be handy.

En Americanus huc equitavit

Én Amèricánus húc
cristátus èquitávit,
et plúmas súpra pósitàs
collýras àppellávit.

Núnc Amèricáne dá
témet rébus béllis:
nùmeróse gráderè:
nunc sálta cúm puéllis!

Núnc ad cástra páter ít
et mécum lègatóque.
Circúmstant ómnes iúvenès
cum grége dènsatóque.

Núnc Amèricáne dá
témet rébus béllis:
nùmeróse gráderè:
nunc sálta cúm puéllis!

---

appellō, āre, āvī, ātum – *to name*
bellus, a, um – *nice*
castra, ōrum, *n.pl.* – *camp*
circumstō, āre, circumstetī – *to stand around*
collȳra, ae, *f.* – *macaroni*
cristātus, a, um – *that has a crest*
densātus, a, um – *thick, crowded*
ēn – *lo and behold!*
equitō, āre, āvī, ātum – *to ride*

gradior, gradī, gressus sum – *to march*
grex, gregis, *m.* – *group of people*
hūc (*adv.*) – *to this place*
iuvenis, iuvenis, *m.* – *young man*
lēgātus, ī, *m.* – *officer*
numerōsē (*adv.*) – *rhythmically*
plūma, ae, *f.* – *feather*
saltō, āre, āvī, ātum – *to dance*
suprā (*adv.*) – *above*
tēmet = tē (*with an emphatic nuance*)

A Guide to the Audio CD